Contents

1

The Toy Train

A. Read the story and answer the questions.

Tom was reading a big blue book. The book was about a toy train. The train came to life. It took Tom around the world.

1. What colour was the book?

_____

2. What was the book about?

_____

3. What came to life?

_____

4. Where did Tom go?

_____

Phonics : B and T

B. ✏️ Print B and b on the lines below.

B

b

C. ✏️ Colour the pictures that begin with the Bb sound.

D. ✏️ Print T and t on the lines below.

T

t

E. ✏️ Colour the pictures that begin with the Tt sound.

Read the story.

The Toy Train

    Bill has a toy train. He takes it out of the box. He puts it together. He flips the switch. It speeds around the track.

F. **Read the five sentences below. Rewrite them on the lines in the correct order.**

- It speeds around the track.
- He puts it together.
- Bill has a toy train.
- He takes it out of the box.
- He flips the switch.

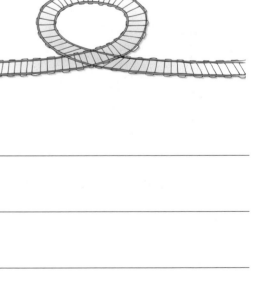

_____

_____

_____

_____

_____

Following Directions

G. **Read the sentences below. Follow the directions.**

> 1. Colour the tent brown.
> 2. Draw three green trees beside the tent.
> 3. Draw five clouds in the sky.
> 4. Draw a yellow sun in the top left corner.

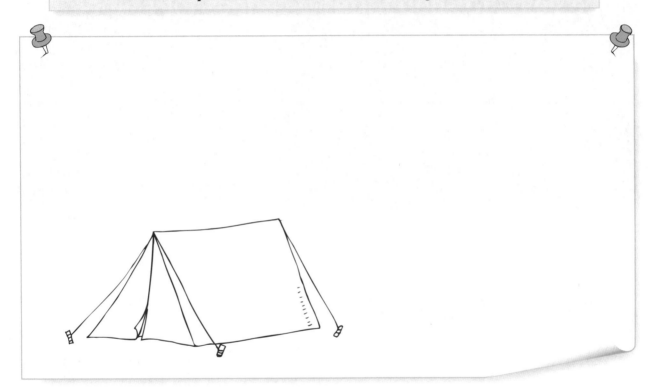

Plurals (1)

H. **Circle ◯ the words that best describe the pictures.**

a ball   balls

a tree      trees

a box   boxes

a tent 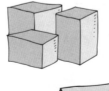   tents

The Shopping Trip

A. Answer the questions.

School is starting soon. Today, my mom and I are going to shop for new clothes for school. I want to buy new socks, slacks and shoes. As a treat, maybe we will have lunch at a restaurant. Shopping for school is fun.

1. What is starting soon?

2. When are they going to shop?

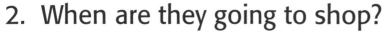

3. What are they shopping for?

4. What is the treat?

B.  **Print C and c on the lines below.**

C

c

C. **Print the letter C under each picture that begins with the Cc sound.**

D. **Print S and s on the lines below.**

S

s

E. **Colour the pictures that begin with the Ss sound.**

Sequencing

F. Look at the pictures. Rewrite the sentences in the correct order.

Baking a cake

We mix the ingredients.
We put the cake in the oven.
We buy the ingredients.
We spread the icing. Yum! Yum!

1. _____

2. _____

3. _____

4. _____

Sentences (1)

G. A sentence begins with a capital letter and ends with a period. Rewrite the following as sentences.

1. the apple is tasty

_____

2. it is sunny outside

_____

3. we went to see our grandparents

_____

4. there are rows and rows of corn

_____

5. we have a pet cat

_____

 Following Directions

H. Read the sentences and complete the picture.

1. Colour the haystack yellow.
2. Draw a big pumpkin beside the haystack.
3. Colour the pumpkin orange.
4. Draw yourself on the right of the haystack.

The New Dog

A. Read the story. In each sentence, circle ( ) the word that fits best.

We have a new dog. His name is Muffy. He has a fluffy grey coat. He likes to play fetch. He sleeps on a blanket beside my bed. I love my new pet.

1. Our new pet is a   cat   dog   turtle .

2. Our pet's name is   Fluffy   Puffy   Muffy .

3. Our pet likes to play   catch   fetch   ball .

4. Our pet sleeps on a   couch   blanket   mat .

5. The colour of our pet's coat is   brown   grey   black .

 Phonics : D and M

B. ✏ Print D and d on the lines below.

D

d

C. ✏️ **Print M and m on the lines below.**

M

m

D. Circle ⬭ the correct beginning sound for each picture.

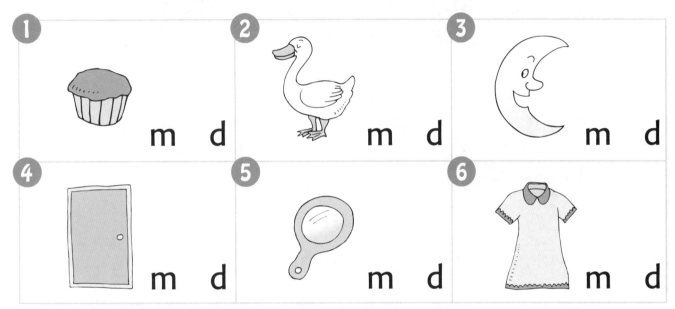

1. m   d

2. m   d

3. m   d

4. m   d

5. m   d

6. m   d

 **Plurals (2)**

E. **For each case, add an "s" to make more than one.**

1. crayon + s =

2. scissor + s =

3. marker + s =

4. block + s =

5. rug + s =

Sequencing

F. Look at the pictures. Rewrite the sentences in order on the lines below.

Moving Day

The movers carried everything onto the truck.
The moving truck came to our house.
The house is empty. Goodbye, house!
The moving truck drove away.

1. _____

2. _____

3. _____

4. _____

Following Directions

G. Read the sentences. Follow the directions.

1. Colour the sun yellow.
2. Colour the barn red.
3. Draw three dogs beside the barn.
4. Draw one pond on each side of the barn.
5. Draw two ducks in each pond.
6. Draw four clouds in the sky.
7. Colour all the animals in the picture.

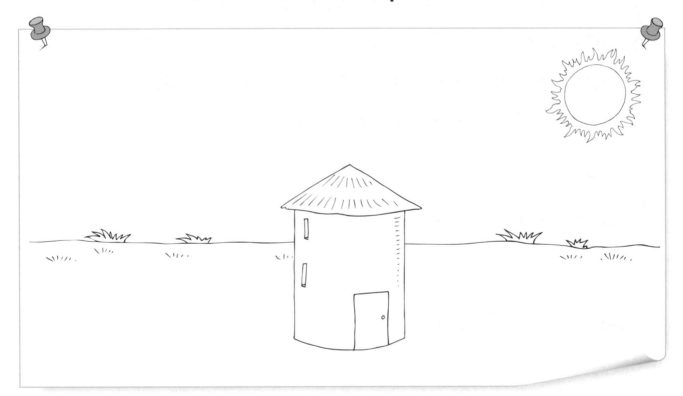

 Extension

1. Get a pencil and some paper.
2. Make up your own set of directions.
3. Read out the directions to a friend.

The Race

A. Read the story and answer the questions.

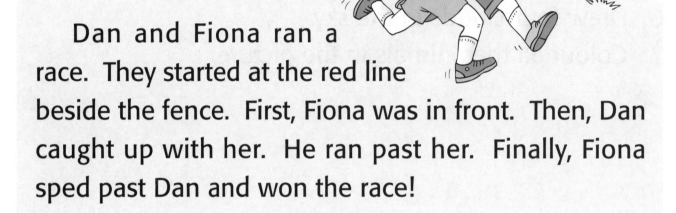

Dan and Fiona ran a race. They started at the red line beside the fence. First, Fiona was in front. Then, Dan caught up with her. He ran past her. Finally, Fiona sped past Dan and won the race!

1. Who ran in the race?

   _____

2. Where did they start?

   _____

3. Who was in the lead at first?

   _____

4. Who won the race?

   _____

Phonics : F and R

B. ✏️ **Print F and f on the lines below.**

F

f

C. ✏️ **Colour the objects that begin with the Ff sound.**

D. ✏️ **Print R and r on the lines below.**

R

r

E. ✏️ **Draw four things that begin with the Rr sound.**

Following Directions

F.   A <u>map</u> helps you find your way around. Look at the map. Follow
     the directions.

1. Draw a house <u>south</u> of the school.

2. Colour the house red.

3. Draw a car on the street that is <u>east</u> of the person.

4. Draw three trees <u>north</u> of the school.

5. Colour the leaves green and the trunk brown.

6. Draw a swimming pool <u>west</u> of the park.

7. Colour the swimming pool blue.

8. Draw yourself in the picture.

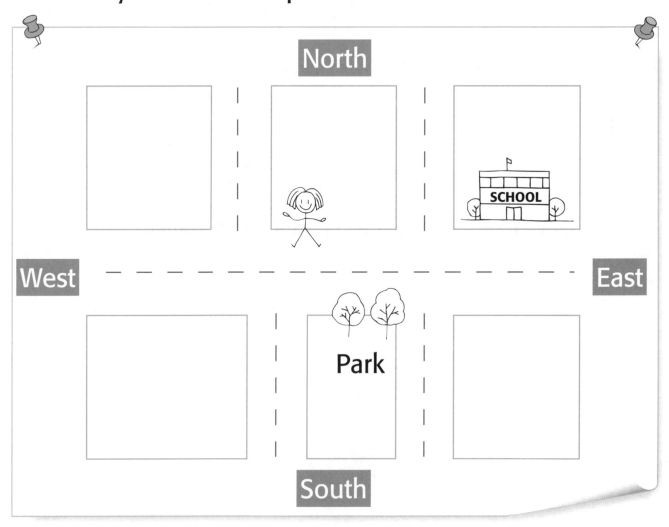

Sentences (2)

- A sentence is a group of words. It tells a complete thought about someone or something.

  Example: The flower is pretty.

  (This tells something about the flower.)

G. Write "yes" for sentences. Write "no" for the rest.

1. the apple tree _____

2. The fire is hot. _____

3. Carrots taste good. _____

4. sweet sugar _____

5. A dog barks. _____

6. man on the moon _____

7. The train chugged along. _____

Cloze

H. The pictures tell about the missing words. Put in your own words that fit the pictures.

1. Roy climbed the _____ to chase the butterfly.

2. Frank swam down the _____ .

3. The _____ burned bright in the camp.

5 Plants

A. Read the story and answer the questions.

Plants are living things.
They make their own food.
They need light and water.
Most plants get their light from the sun and their water from the rain. Light and water make plants grow.

1. What are plants?

   _____

2. Who makes food for plants?

   _____

3. What two things do plants need?

   _____

4. Where do most plants get their light?

   _____

5. Where do most plants get their water?

   _____

Phonics: G and P

B. 🖊 **Print G and g on the lines below.**

C. 🖊 **Print the letter g under each picture that begins with the Gg sound.**

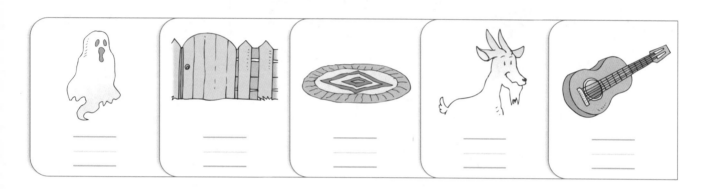

D. 🖊 **Print P and p on the lines below.**

E. 🖍 **Colour the pictures in the pizza slices that begin with the Pp sound.**

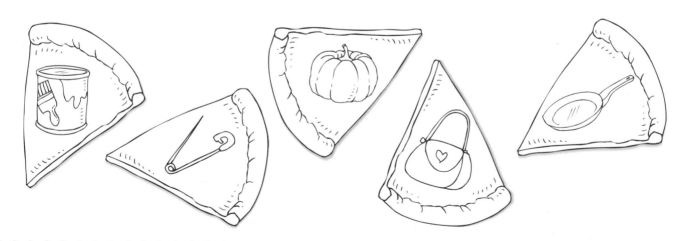

Sequencing

F. Look at the pictures and read the sentences. Rewrite the sentences in the order of the pictures.

We dig the soil.
The plant sprouts.
It rains; then the sun shines.
We buy the seeds.
We plant the seeds.

1. _____

2. _____

3. _____

4. _____

5. _____

Sentences (3)

- A sentence is a group of words that tells a complete thought about someone or something.

    Example: The boy jumps.

G. Look at the pictures. Read the sentences. Print the numbers of the sentences in the picture boxes.

1. There are lots of vegetables.
2. The pig squeals.
3. The goose laid a golden egg.
4. The pizza has pepperoni on it.
5. The pillow is soft.
6. The penguin lives in Antarctica.
7. There are three balloons.
8. The bell is ringing.
9. The goat has a kid.

The Witch

A. Read the story. Circle ○ the correct answers.

Judy is a friendly witch. She wears magic jumping boots. She likes to jump over trees and houses. When Judy jumps, people watch. She wishes she could jump over the moon, but her jumping boots won't go that high.

1. Judy is a _____ witch.

   mean   fearless   friendly

2. Judy wears magic _____ .

   shoes   hats   boots

3. She likes to jump over _____ .

   trees   bushes   haystacks

4. When Judy jumps, people _____ .

   wait   watch   wish

5. Judy wishes she could jump over the _____ .

   cow   moon   houses

B. Print W and w on the lines below.

W

w

C. Draw the pictures that begin with the Ww sound inside the web.

D. Print J and j on the lines below.

J

j

E. Colour the pictures that begin with the Jj sound.

F. Look at the pictures and read the sentences. Rewrite the sentences in the order of the pictures.

Pour the batter into the pan.

Mix the ingredients.

Eat the cake. Yum!

Bake the cake in the oven.

Shop for all the ingredients.

1. _____

2. _____

3. _____

4. _____

5. _____

Following Directions

G. Read the sentences. Follow the directions.

1. Draw two candles in the window on the top floor.

2. Draw one door in the middle of the bottom floor.

3. Draw three jack-o'-lanterns in the windows.
4. Draw four ghosts in the garden.
5. Draw a witch in the house.
6. Draw a blue moon in the sky.

Question Words

- *Some sentences ask about someone or something. These are questions.*
- *Some questions begin with these words.*

  Who   What   Where   When   Why   How

H. Read the groups of words. Choose the words that make sense.

1. _____ are you going? | Who Where

2. _____ is your new teacher? | What Who

3. _____ will you go home? | Where When

4. _____ will you wear today? | When What

5. _____ did you break the toy? | What Why

Hens and Chicks

A. Read the story and answer the questions.

Dear Ned,

   How are you? I have been
learning all about chicks and hens. Did you know that
chickens are birds? Hens lay eggs and sit on them to
warm them. A baby chick grows inside the egg. Then
the chick pecks at the shell when it is ready to hatch.
Pop! A new baby chick is born.

Your friend,
Harry

1. What has Harry been learning about?

_____

2. What kind of animal is a chicken?

_____

3. Where do baby chicks grow before they are hatched?

_____

4. How do baby chicks get hatched?

_____

5. Who will get this letter?

_____

Phonics: H and N

B. Print H and h on the lines below.

H

h

C. Colour the pictures that begin with the Hh sound.

D. Print N and n on the lines below.

N

n

E. Circle ◯ the correct beginning sound for each picture.

1.	h / n	2.	h / n	3.	h / n	4.	h / n
5.	h / n	6.	h / n	7.	h / n	8.	h / n

Sequencing

F. Look at the pictures and read the sentences. Rewrite the sentences in the order of the pictures.

The baby chick pecks at the shell.
The chick hatches from the shell.
The hen lays an egg.
The hen sits on the egg to warm it.

1. _____

2. _____

3. _____

4. _____

Spelling

G. Circle ◯ the correct word in each row.

1.	chicken	cicken	chickn	chiccken
2.	htch	hatch	haetch	heatch
3.	pecks	pcks	peks	peacks

Sentences (4)

- *Some sentences tell about someone or something.*
- *Some sentences ask about someone or something.*

H. **For each case, circle ◯ the "T" if the sentence is a telling sentence. Circle ◯ the "A" if the sentence is an asking sentence.**

1. Have you seen the horse?   T A

2. We have a new teacher.   T A

3. How did he fall?   T A

4. She went to school.   T A

5. I like to play hopscotch.   T A

 Following Directions

I. **Read the sentences and complete the picture.**

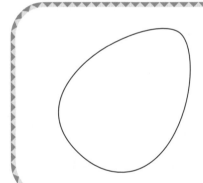 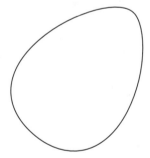 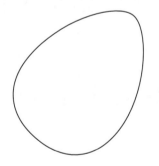

1. Draw a straight red line in the centre of the first egg.

2. Draw a blue line on each side of the red line.

3. Colour the second egg yellow.

4. Draw a design on the third egg.

5. Colour the third egg in your favourite colour.

8 Kites

A. Read the sign and answer the questions.

Let's go fly a kite, up to the sky so bright.
Let's go fly a kite and send it soaring.

Kites for sale

boxes, diamonds, dragons and more ...
Prices start at $5.00.

1. What is the sign selling?

   _____

2. What shapes are the kites?

   _____

3. What is so bright ?

   _____

4. What is the starting price of the kites?

   _____

5. How many times does the word "kite(s)" appear on the sign?

   _____

Phonics: K and V

B. Print K and k on the lines below.

K

k

C. Connect the dots beside the pictures of the words that begin with the Kk sound.

D. Print V and v on the lines below.

V

v

E. Find these words in the word search.

vine   van   vest   violin   valentine

B	D	U	X	C	O	L	V	M	T	R	S	V	A	V	K	M	F	H
Q	C	F	H	I	E	V	A	L	E	N	T	I	N	E	G	I	L	K
T	V	I	O	L	I	N	W	F	S	V	A	N	Z	S	T	U	R	S
L	A	I	R	A	I	N	R	R	E	T	B	E	O	T	O	V	R	N

Sequencing

F. Read the story and the instructions. Rewrite the instructions in the correct order.

Making a Kite

Today we made a kite. We bought sticks, paper, glue, and string. Kathleen cut the paper into a diamond shape. Next, Val cut the string. Then, Keith cut the sticks. Finally, we glued the sticks to the paper and added the string. Then we flew our kite.

Instructions

Fly the kite.
Buy the paper, sticks, glue, and string.
Glue the sticks and string to the paper.
Cut the paper, sticks, and string.

1. _____

2. _____

3. _____

4. _____

Following Directions

G. **Read the sentences and complete the picture.**

1. Draw three valentines.
2. Colour one valentine red.
3. Colour one valentine purple.
4. Colour one valentine pink.
5. Draw a kite beside the purple valentine.

Nouns (1)

• *Some nouns name people.*

H. **Underline the nouns that name the people in these sentences.**

1. The teacher told a story.

2. A fireman wears a helmet.

3. A nurse helps sick people.

4. A baker makes cookies and cakes.

5. The police officer drove a motorcycle.

Comprehension / Sequencing

A. Read the story and write the sentences in the correct order.

Making a Tent

My brother and I wanted to make a tent. First, we went to ask our mom for an old blanket. Then we got some clothespins. We took everything out to the backyard. We hung the blanket over the clothesline. Finally, we pinned the blanket to the line with clothespins. Now we are cozy inside our tent.

We asked our mom for an old blanket.
We are cozy inside our tent.
We took everything out to the backyard.
We got some clothespins.
We pinned the blanket to the clothesline.

1. _____

2. _____

3. _____

4. _____

5. _____

Phonics

B. Look at each picture. Write the beginning letter for it in the word box below it.

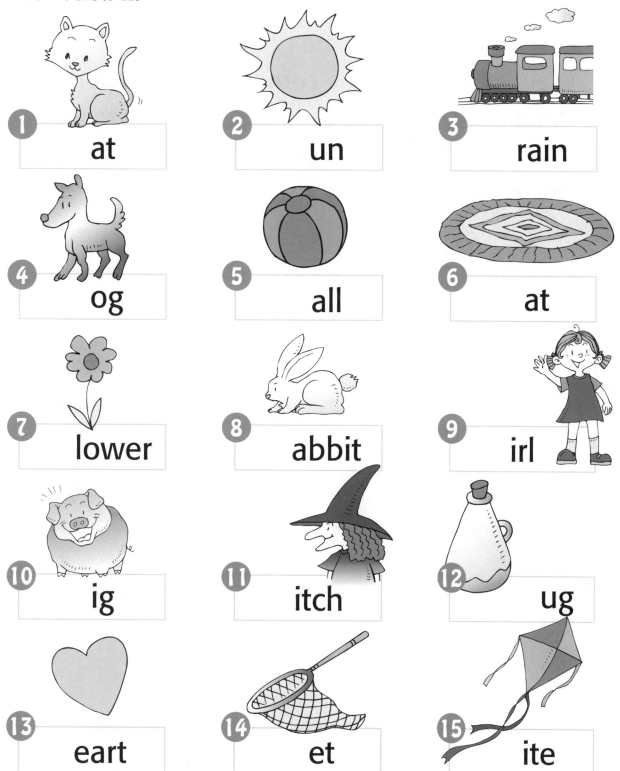

1 at

2 un

3 rain

4 og

5 all

6 at

7 lower

8 abbit

9 irl

10 ig

11 itch

12 ug

13 eart

14 et

15 ite

C. Read the sentences. Follow the directions.

1. Draw a house in the corner above the road.
2. Draw three ducks in the pond.
3. Draw four trees in the corner above the pond.
4. Draw a car with two people in it on the road.
5. Draw two children and one ball in the corner below the road.

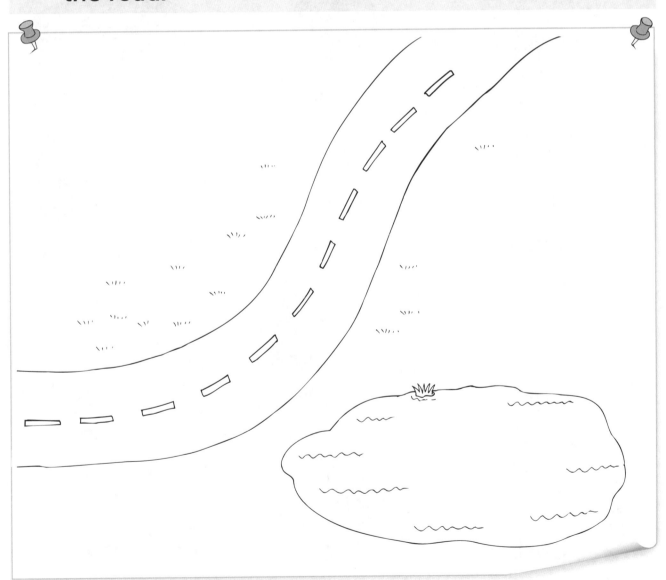

Word Search

D. Find the words and circle ( ) them.

saw	carrot	tent	ball	cat	dog	moon	flower
goat	pizza	witch	jam	heart	nest	kite	van rug

K	Y	S	U	B	B	L	M	E	S	Z	O	D	B	F	F	A
U	J	X	X	C	W	N	D	H	T	F	K	P	I	Z	Z	A
U	C	C	A	R	R	O	T	H	C	O	F	D	G	E	I	U
D	Y	K	H	M	O	G	U	J	L	O	X	A	S	N	Z	E
E	E	O	G	S	S	K	I	T	E	T	S	C	A	T	H	L
U	S	T	H	H	F	G	I	H	T	X	Y	M	F	E	V	O
O	F	L	O	W	E	R	R	U	G	U	U	D	S	N	D	C
K	N	D	G	C	E	S	K	F	M	T	R	W	S	T	S	D
H	E	A	R	T	T	O	E	U	E	C	B	D	O	G	F	S
L	S	Y	O	M	C	U	K	F	E	U	J	C	C	O	N	D
D	Y	G	O	A	T	E	C	A	S	F	N	A	S	C	H	W
P	M	S	V	G	L	T	C	O	A	B	R	G	H	S	F	E
R	T	S	C	M	O	O	N	O	W	I	T	C	H	O	B	C
S	S	K	E	Z	Z	N	V	H	C	A	E	N	R	O	W	T
A	J	U	E	F	W	P	A	W	I	O	V	B	A	L	L	P
C	N	E	S	T	M	D	L	C	J	A	M	Y	N	W	J	K
D	T	G	W	O	G	E	N	S	E	H	T	E	R	A	O	M
R	F	I	E	M	O	J	T	U	S	E	C	H	V	A	N	C

Plurals

E. Circle ◯ the word that best describes each picture.

1	2	3
a bee / bees	a cup / cups	a cat / cats

4	5	6
a sock / socks	a fan / fans	the moon / moons

7	8	9
a dog / dogs	a pig / pigs	a hat / hats

Sentences

F. Rewrite these groups of words as sentences.

> A sentence is a group of words. Some sentences tell about someone or something and end with periods. Some sentences ask questions and end with question marks.

1. went Bill zoo. the to
2. park. at fun We the had
3. store? Will go you the to
4. to school? How go do you
5. Kate friend My with plays me.
6. coming my to When you are house?
7. are lots rabbits There pet of store. at the
8. cake The baking the oven. is in

1. _____

2. _____

3. _____

4. _____

5. _____

6. _____

7. _____

8. _____

Living at the Zoo

A. Read the story and answer the questions.

Hi! My name is Zoey. I am a two-year-old zebra. I live at the zoo with my parents, Lily and Luther. Before I was born, my mom and dad came to the zoo from Africa. We like to lie in the warm sun.

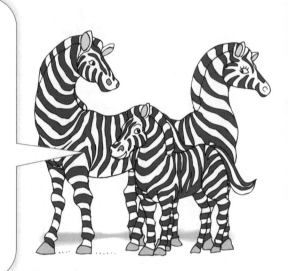

1. What kind of animal is Zoey?

   _____

2. Where does Zoey live?

   _____

3. Who are Zoey's parents?

   _____

4. When did Zoey's parents come to live at the zoo?

   _____

5. What does Zoey like to do?

   _____

Phonics: L and Z

B. 🖊 Print L and l on the lines below.

L

l

C. 🖊 Print Z and z on the lines below.

Z

z

D. 🖍 Colour the pictures blue if they begin with the Ll sound. Colour the pictures red if they begin with the Zz sound.

Sequencing

E. Look at the pictures and read the sentences. Rewrite the sentences in the order of the pictures.

Finally, I hang my picture on the wall.

First, I colour my picture.

Next, I glue my picture to the construction paper.

Then I cut my picture out.

1. _____

2. _____

3. _____

4. _____

Following Directions

F. Draw the following zoo animals above their names.

a zebra	an elephant	a lion

Rhyming Words

- *Words that sound the same at the end are rhyming words.*

G. Read each word and write a word that rhymes with it.

1. Boo! _____
2. hand _____
3. sad _____
4. seed _____
5. me _____
6. bag _____
7. money _____
8. house _____
9. tree _____
10. man _____

Nouns (2)

- *Some nouns name places.*

H. Read each sentence. Underline the noun that names a place.

1. Last summer, we went to the zoo.

2. We will go to the store after lunch.

3. Some zebras come from South Africa.

4. The whales live in the ocean.

5. The park has swings.

6. Our classroom is filled with pictures and maps.

7. The oranges are in the kitchen.

8. We visited a farm on our vacation.

The Fox and the Queen

Read the story.

A queen came upon a fox in the royal wood. She questioned the fox about its home. The fox was cunning. He questioned the queen about her palace. She answered his questions. Late at night, while the palace slept, the fox crept in and stole a box with all of the crown jewels in it. Poor sad queen!

A.   Fill in the blanks with words from the story.

The 1._____ and the 2._____

The 3._____ came upon the 4._____ in the royal 5._____. The fox 6._____ the 7._____ about her 8._____ . The queen answered his 9._____ . The fox was 10._____ . He crept into the 11._____ . While everyone 12._____ , he stole a 13._____ with the 14._____ in it.

B.   Answer the questions.

1. When did the fox steal the jewels?

_____

2. Where did the queen live?

_____

3. How did the fox know where to find the jewels?

_____

 Phonics: Q and X

C. ✏ **Print Q and q on the lines below.**

Q

q

D. ✏ **Print X and x on the lines below.**

X

x

E. ✏ **Colour the pictures blue if they begin with the Qq sound. Colour the pictures red if they end with the Xx sound.**

Sequencing

F. Read the story and read the sentences. Rewrite the sentences in the correct order.

Ride a Bike

I want to ride my new bike. I put on my helmet. I take the bike out to the sidewalk. I put one leg over the top to sit down. I place my feet on the pedals. Away I go!

Put one leg over the top.
Take the bike out to the sidewalk.
Put on a helmet.
Place your feet on the pedals.

1. _____

2. _____

3. _____

4. _____

Following Directions

G. Read the sentences. Follow the directions.

1. Colour the box green.

2. Draw a smaller box to the right of the green box. Colour it blue.

3. Draw a box bigger than the green one under the blue box.

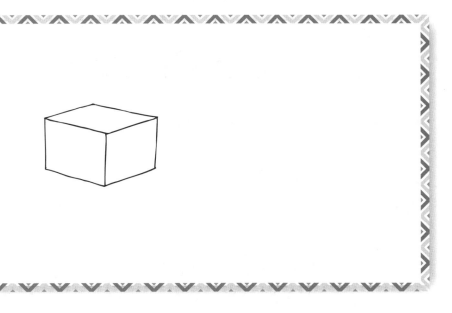

Nouns (3)

- *Some nouns name one person or thing. These are singular nouns.*
- *Some nouns name more than one person or thing. These are plural nouns.*

H. Circle ◯ the noun that fits best in each sentence.

1. The police officer wears a blue hats / hat .

2. The nurse works in a hospitals / hospital .

3. The mouse ran up the clock / clocks .

4. The boy likes his schools / school .

5. The pilot lands his airplane / airplanes .

6. The girl likes green apple / apples best.

7. The babies want their bottles / bottle .

8. They wrapped all the box / boxes with giftwrap.

9. On the street, there are lots of cars / car .

10. The markers / marker are on the table.

The Wild Yak

A. Read the story and answer the questions.

The wild yak is a large ox. It lives in a place called Tibet. A yak can grow to be 1.8 metres tall. A wild yak has long black hair. It has long horns on its head. It eats grass.

1. What type of animal is a wild yak?

_____

2. Where does the wild yak live?

_____

3. What does the wild yak eat?

_____

4. What colour is its hair?

_____

5. How tall are some yaks?

_____

B. ✏️ **Print Y and y on the lines below.**

Y

y

C. **Draw a line from the Y in the yo-yo to each picture that begins with the Yy sound.**

Sequencing

D. Look at the pictures and read the sentences. Rewrite the sentences in the order of the pictures.

I let the yo-yo fall.

I have a yo-yo.

My yo-yo goes up and down.

I wind the string around my yo-yo.

1. _____

2. _____

3. _____

4. _____

Word Order in Sentences

- *Some sentences begin with capital letters and end with periods.*
- *Sentences make sense.*

E. Read the mixed-up sentences. Rewrite them on the lines below them. Add the appropriate punctuation marks.

Example: apple is The juicy

The apple is juicy.

1. A long horns wild has yak

_____

2. hat is in Your box the

_____

3. smile a have You pretty

_____

4. need yellow I crayon a

_____

5. cage bird sings The a in

_____

6. is yummy banana It a

_____

7. my Look dog at cute

_____

8. like play to I with dog my

_____

The Tree-house

Hello! My name is Robert. In the summer, I built a tree-house. I got some wood, some nails, and a hammer. My dad helped me put the tree-house together. We built it in the big tree in our backyard. It is fun to play with my friends there.

A. **Answer the questions.**

1. What is the name of the boy in the story?

   _____

2. What did the boy build with his father?

   _____

3. What did they use to build it?

   _____

4. Where did they build it?

   _____

5. When did they build it?

   _____

B.   Write 'a', 'e', 'i', 'o' or 'u' in each box.   Then read out the words.

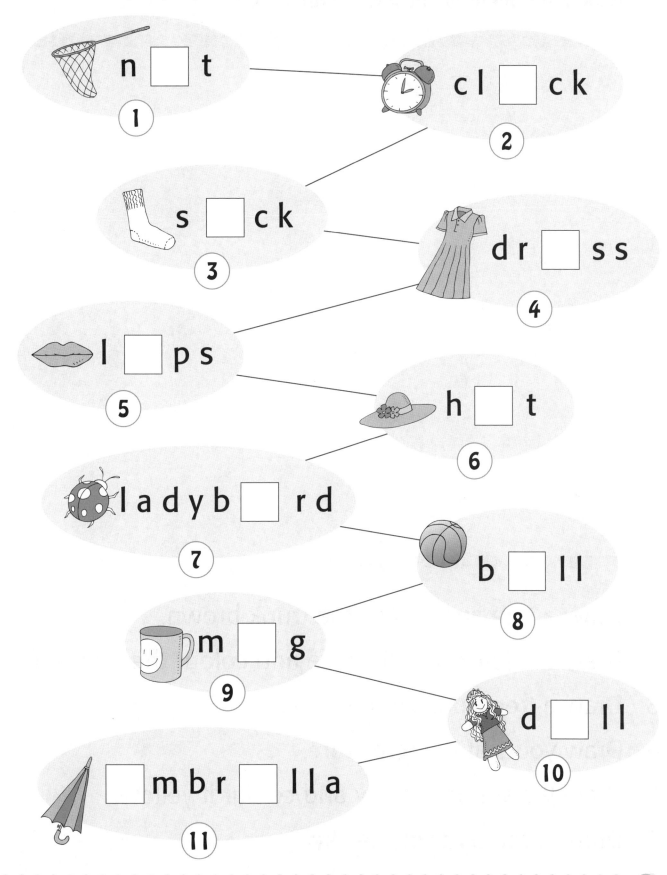

n ☐ t
1

cl ☐ ck
2

s ☐ ck
3

dr ☐ ss
4

l ☐ ps
5

h ☐ t
6

ladyb ☐ rd
7

b ☐ ll
8

m ☐ g
9

d ☐ ll
10

☐ mbr ☐ lla
11

Following Directions

C. Read the sentences. Follow the directions.

1. Draw a tree and colour the trunk brown.

2. Draw the leaves on the tree and colour them green.

3. Draw a tree-house in the tree.

4. Draw yourself in the picture.

5. Draw the sun in the sky and colour it yellow.

6. Draw some birds in the sky.

Sentence Structures

D. Read the following groups of words. Put the words in the correct order to make sentences. Write the sentences on the lines below.

1. flowers   are   bloom.   The   in

_____

2. are   skates?   my   Where

_____

3. very   dress   The   pretty.   is

_____

4. many   bluebirds   There   are   sky.   the   in

_____

Synonyms

• *Synonyms are words that have the same meaning.*

E. Circle ◯ the synonyms of the words in the grey boxes.

1.	below	in	down	inside	out
2.	up	down	out	big	above
3.	big	over	under	large	outside
4.	small	tiny	big	huge	tall

The Bat

A. Read the story. Fill in the blanks.

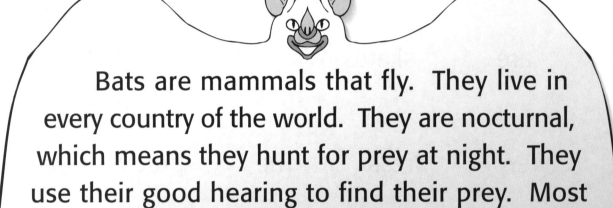

Bats are mammals that fly. They live in every country of the world. They are nocturnal, which means they hunt for prey at night. They use their good hearing to find their prey. Most bats like to eat insects.

1. Bats are _____ that _____ .

2. Bats live in every _____ of the _____ .

3. Bats are _____ , which means they _____ for prey at _____ .

4. Bats have good _____ .

5. Most bats eat _____ .

Ending Sounds: T, B and D

B. Print the letters that name the ending sounds.

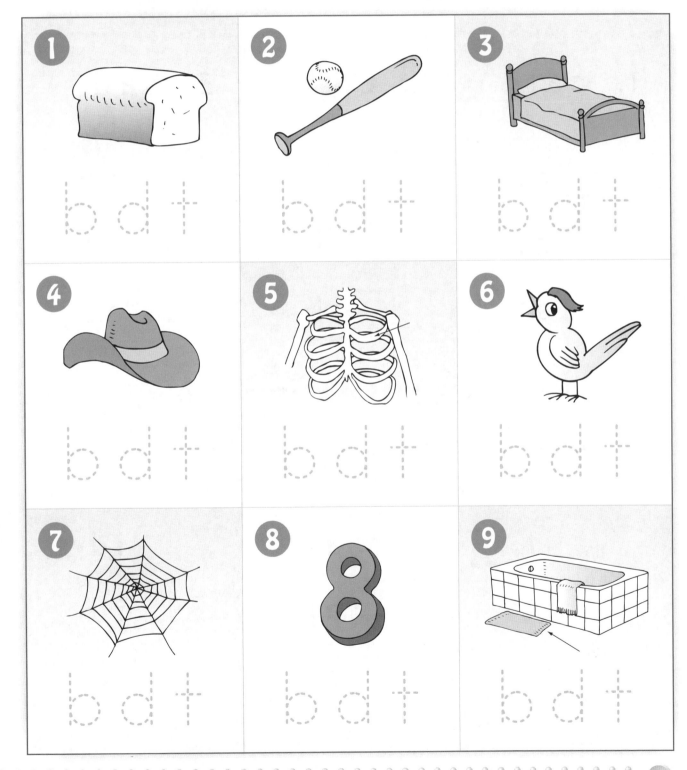

Word Families

C. Read the word at the top of each column. Print the words that are from the same word family.

They sound the same at the end.

1. c a t	2. c r i b	3. s a d
☐ a t	☐ i b	☐ a d
☐ a t	☐ i b	☐ a d
☐ a t	☐ i b	☐ a d

4. s i t	5. c a p	6. l i d
☐ i t	☐ a p	☐ i d
☐ i t	☐ a p	☐ i d
☐ i t	☐ a p	☐ i d

Inflections and Endings

D. Fill in the correct words in the blanks.

1. The dog _____ at the mail carrier.
   bark, barked

2. The girl will _____ now.
   start, started

3. Robert is _____ his guitar.
   play, playing

4. David is a good _____ .
   dancer, dancers

5. Kathleen _____ a lot.
   talks, talking

6. Her _____ is Mary.
   name, names

7. She is _____ muffins.
   bake, baking

8. We _____ to the zoo yesterday.
   go, went

9. Where will she _____ the race?
   run, ran

10. Jim is a _____ runner than Bill.
    good, better

Making Blueberry Jam

A. Read the instructions. Answer the questions.

My mom and I are going to make blueberry jam. First, we go to our secret place to pick blueberries from the bushes. Then we sit and pick all the blueberries we want. When we get home, we clean the berries, taking out the leaves. Mom puts them in a pot with water and sugar and boils it on the stove. When it is cooled, we taste it. Yum! Yum!

1. What is the first thing to do to make blueberry jam?

_____

2. Where do they go to pick berries?

_____

3. What do they do after they bring the berries home?

_____

Ending Sounds: M, F and R

B.  Colour the pictures in each group that end with the sound of the letter.

drum
ja r
scarf

m

f

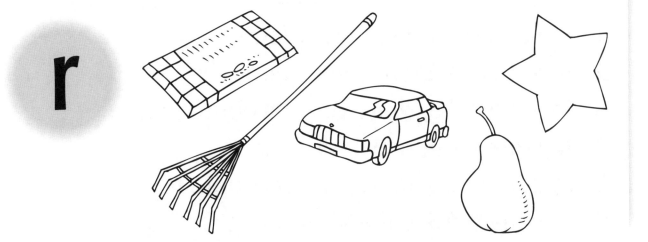

r

C. Read the sentences. Follow the directions.

1. In square #1, draw your family.
2. In square #2, draw your house.
3. In square #3, draw your favourite pet.
4. In square #4, draw your car.
5. In square #5, draw your favourite toy.
6. In square #6, write your name.

Antonyms

- Antonyms are words that are opposites.

  Examples: hot ⟶ cold
              up ⟶ down

D. Circle ◯ the antonym of the first word in each row.

1.	hard	rough	soft	slimy
2.	stop	red	look	go
3.	night	day	week	time
4.	white	blue	green	black
5.	she	you	he	I
6.	no	maybe	was	yes
7.	happy	sad	feel	fun
8.	big	wide	little	huge
9.	asleep	time	night	awake
10.	we	it	they	he

15 Pretty Lights

A. Read the poem and answer the questions.

When I see them, they're such pretty lights.

I can see them in the night time.

When it's dark out, they look nice.

I like the pretty lights.

1. What is the poem about?

   _____

2. What time of day is the writer talking about?

   _____

3. Do you think the lights are in the country or the city?

   _____

4. Do you ever see pretty lights? Where?

   _____

Ending Sounds : L, P and N

B. Draw a line from each letter to the picture that ends with the sound of that letter.

Filling in Speech Bubbles

C. Fill in the words that you think these characters are saying to each other.

Crossword Puzzle

D. Read the clues and complete the crossword puzzle.

Down
1. flying mammal that hunts at night
2. pet that purrs
3. used to gather cut grass

Across
A. what rabbits like to eat
B. place to sleep when camping
C. Let's go fly a _____.

Verbs

- *Verbs are action words.*
  Example: Mary <u>plays</u> with her dolls.

E. Underline the verbs in these sentences.

1. Jim rides his bike.

2. David plays the guitar.

3. Kathleen looks at the stars.

4. Rob works at school.

5. Mary cooks her dinner.

6. Dad baked a cake.

7. They walked to the store.

8. The girls jumped the rope.

9. Christina skates every week.

10. Ryan likes baseball.

16 *What Am I?*

A.   Read the sentences in each group.   Circle ◯ the correct word.

1. I am round.
    I make a sound.
    You use sticks to play me.
    What am I?

    a doll   a drum   a guitar   a ball

2. I am hot.
    I look yellow.
    I heat the Earth.
    What am I?

    the sun   the star
    the sky   the moon

3. I am round.
    I can bounce.
    I can roll.
    What am I?

    a ball   a book
    a doll   a flower

4. I am round.
    I am made of metal.
    You can buy things with me.
    What am I?

    a coin   a candle
    a crane   a carrot

5. I can be hard.
    I can be soft.
    You read me.
    What am I?

    a book   a box
    a hook   a doll

Ending Sounds : G, K and S

B. Colour the pictures that end with the sound of each letter.

Word Search

C. Find these words in the word search. Highlight them with a yellow crayon.

stop   children   coin   bat   turtle   leave

trees   tomorrow   light   hop   today   school

D	C	A	K	Y	G	U	O	M	X	H	D	F	V	I
E	U	B	L	N	P	E	W	Q	I	T	R	E	E	S
B	X	N	R	R	A	K	V	O	M	U	K	X	N	N
U	E	G	F	O	C	H	I	L	D	R	E	N	T	Y
C	S	J	U	X	O	M	J	D	E	T	A	U	R	B
N	Y	S	T	M	I	R	O	T	W	L	I	G	H	T
W	T	U	J	F	N	E	C	H	J	E	O	C	L	V
K	U	B	A	J	Y	F	L	C	N	S	E	V	O	I
T	X	K	L	A	V	C	N	E	D	B	G	H	P	S
U	T	T	O	M	O	R	R	O	W	S	C	L	O	D
R	E	O	F	B	C	A	C	L	E	V	Y	E	G	E
V	K	D	R	L	H	G	O	C	A	C	F	A	S	R
M	O	A	U	I	V	D	J	H	F	R	A	V	S	M
S	D	Y	N	C	S	C	H	O	O	L	U	E	B	I
T	A	V	B	A	T	J	S	P	L	D	T	S	U	A
E	D	I	F	V	O	T	N	S	L	X	N	H	O	Z
K	C	B	O	F	P	E	E	D	U	F	G	L	X	N

Rhyming Words

- *Words that rhyme sound the same at the end.*
  Example: cat   bat   sat

D. Circle ◯ the word in each row that rhymes with the first word.

1.	hot	cold	honey	pot	cat
2.	go	to	gone	so	fun
3.	run	here	fun	tag	walk
4.	tag	game	it	bag	play
5.	red	bed	stop	blue	round
6.	mug	cup	rug	hot	bold
7.	sit	down	up	at	it
8.	man	ran	woman	boy	out
9.	book	hard	read	ton	hook
10.	cake	eat	bake	ice	lunch

Fun at School

A. Read what the girl says. Answer the questions.

We do lots of fun things at school. We play games to learn new words. We count teddy bear cookies. We draw and paint pictures. We play games on the computer. I like my school.

1. Which place is this girl talking about?

_____

2. How does she learn new words?

_____

3. What does she count?

_____

4. What does she paint?

_____

5. How does she feel about school?

_____

Phonics : Beginning and Ending Sounds

B. Look at the pictures. Fill in the missing letters for each word.

1.

☐ u ☐

2.

☐ a ☐

3.

☐ e ☐

4.

☐ o ☐

5.

☐ a l ☐

6.

☐ e n ☐

7.
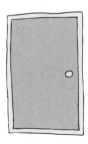
☐ r u ☐

8.

☐ a ☐

9.

☐ i r ☐

10.
☐ o o ☐

11.
☐ a ☐

12.
☐ a ☐

Word Search

C. **Find the following words in the word search. Put a line through each word when you find it.**

box	ball	doll	cat	bad	bib
cot	drum	bird	pan	door	bed
cup	hat	cap	top	bag	tent

X	J	M	K	O	I	A	X	M	D	O	R	L
C	A	P	F	H	B	K	S	N	O	B	M	W
U	T	N	G	D	O	L	L	T	N	A	C	F
P	B	L	H	O	X	A	N	M	N	D	C	M
U	I	O	T	O	U	F	C	R	T	Q	J	Q
V	R	F	U	R	L	P	Q	D	V	W	V	F
X	D	B	H	T	A	A	F	R	J	B	A	G
T	N	G	D	H	U	N	Q	U	X	I	V	N
R	O	Y	X	A	M	P	C	M	O	B	H	B
S	T	E	N	T	J	Y	N	X	I	T	R	E
C	K	V	R	N	W	B	A	L	L	G	E	D
O	L	X	S	U	F	C	P	E	F	W	B	X
T	O	P	C	A	T	I	G	H	G	T	D	A

D. Fill in the correct word in each sentence.

1. We _____ play, played at the park
    yesterday.

2. She _____ was, were the best
    dancer there.

3. He _____ give, gave them some
    gum.

4. You _____ will, did go with them
    tomorrow.

5. She _____ want, wanted to eat the
    candy.

6. It _____ rained, rain all day today.

7. We _____ had, has a good time
    singing.

8. They _____ will, were play at
    school.

9. The car _____ stop, stopped at the
    red light.

10. Kathleen _____ dance, danced all
    night long.

Comprehension

A.   Read the story and answer the questions.

My Favourite Hobby

My favourite hobby is collecting rocks. From the Spring to the Fall, I go for long walks with my mom and we stop and pick up rocks along the way on the sides of the roads and on paths. All the rocks are different. Some have spots, some have stripes and others have many colours. Some are pink, some are blue and some are grey or black. I have 123 rocks in my collection now.

1. What is the boy's favourite hobby?

   _____

2. With whom does he go for long walks?

   _____

3. When does he collect the rocks?

   _____

4. Where do they find the rocks?

   _____

5. How do the rocks look?

   _____

6. How many rocks does he have in his collection?

_____

B. Look at each picture. Fill in the missing vowel.

1 c [ ] t	**2** l [ ] p s	**3** l [ ] g
4 h [ ] n d	**5** r [ ] g	**6** b [ ] l l
7 s [ ] x	**8** d [ ] g	**9** c [ ] p
10 t [ ] p	**11** t [ ] n t	**12** f [ ] s h

C. Circle ◯ the beginning sound of each picture.

D. **Find the phrase that matches each word. Draw a line to connect them.**

hat		something to cook in
cat		an adult human male
bat		something to wear on your head
man		made of a metal, like tin
fan		an animal with whiskers and a long tail
can		a flying mammal
van		it keeps you cool in summer
pan		a fish has one
fin		it carries a lot of people

E. **Solve the riddles.**

1. What's black and white and read all over?
   _____

2. What rises in the East and sets in the West?
   _____

F. **Read the sentences below. Put them in the correct order. Add an ending of your own.**

Making an Ice Cream Cone

I like to make ice cream cones. My favourite flavour is strawberry. First, I go to the cupboard and take a cone from the package. Then, I get the ice cream from the freezer. I use a scoop to pick up the ice cream and place it on top of the cone. Finally, I put some sprinkles on top.

Get the ice cream out of the freezer.
Use a scoop to pick up the ice cream.
Put some sprinkles on top.
Go to the cupboard.
Get out a cone.

1. _____

2. _____

3. _____

4. _____

5. _____

Add an ending of your own.

6. _____

Nouns and Verbs

G. Underline the nouns and circle ◯ the verbs in the sentences below.

1. The boy rode his bike to the store.

2. The kite flew high into the sky.

3. Cats like to play with yarn.

4. Babies cry when they want to be fed.

5. Libby drives a car to work.

6. David plays the guitar well.

7. Kathleen runs on the track at school.

8. Rob buys cat food at the pet store.

9. Christina looked for her mom everywhere.

10. Ryan rode his new scooter on the sidewalk.

Nouns name a person, place, or thing. Verbs are action words.

1 **The Toy Train**

A. 1. Blue.
2. A toy train.
3. The train.
4. Around the world.

C.

E.

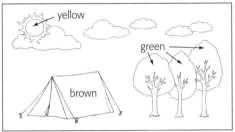

F. Bill has a toy train.
He takes it out of the box.
He puts it together.
He flips the switch.
It speeds around the track.

G. (Suggestions only)

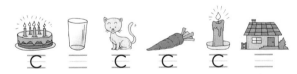

H. a ball ; trees ; boxes ; a tent

2 **The Shopping Trip**

A. 1. School.
2. Today.
3. New clothes.
4. Lunch at a restaurant.

C.

E.

F. 1. We buy the ingredients.
2. We mix the ingredients.
3. We put the cake in the oven.
4. We spread the icing. Yum! Yum!

G. 1. The apple is tasty.
2. It is sunny outside.
3. We went to see our grandparents.
4. There are rows and rows of corn.
5. We have a pet cat.

H. (Suggestions only)

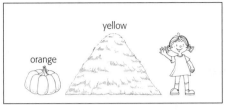

3 **The New Dog**

A. 1. dog 2. Muffy
3. fetch 4. blanket
5. grey

D. 1. m 2. d
3. m 4. d
5. m 6. d

E. 1. crayons 2. scissors
3. markers 4. blocks
5. rugs

F. 1. The moving truck came to our house.
2. The movers carried everything onto the truck.
3. The moving truck drove away.
4. The house is empty. Goodbye, house!

G. (Suggestions only)

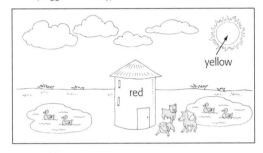

4 **The Race**

A. 1. Dan and Fiona.
2. At the red line beside the fence.
3. Fiona.
4. Fiona.

C.

E. (Individual drawing)
F. (Suggestions only)

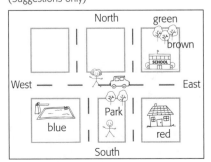

G. 1. no   2. yes   3. yes   4. no
    5. yes   6. no   7. yes
H. 1. fence   2. river
    3. fire

5 Plants

A. 1. Living things.
    2. They make their own food.
    3. Light and water.
    4. From the sun.
    5. From the rain.

C.

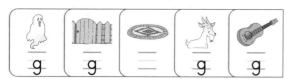

E.

F. 1. We buy the seeds.
    2. We dig the soil.
    3. We plant the seeds.
    4. It rains; then the sun shines.
    5. The plant sprouts.

G.

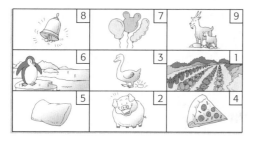

6 The Witch

A. 1. friendly   2. boots
    3. trees   4. watch
    5. moon

C.

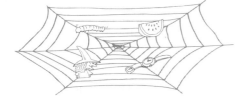

E.

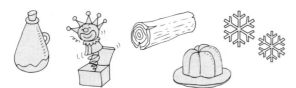

F. 1. Shop for all the ingredients.
    2. Mix the ingredients.

---

    3. Pour the batter into the pan.
    4. Bake the cake in the oven.
    5. Eat the cake. Yum!
G. (Suggestions only)

H. 1. Where   2. Who
    3. When   4. What
    5. Why

7 Hens and Chicks

A. 1. Chicks and hens.
    2. A bird.
    3. Inside eggs.
    4. Hens sit on the eggs to warm them.
    5. Ned.

C.

E. 1. n   2. n   3. h   4. h
    5. n   6. n   7. h   8. n
F. 1. The hen lays an egg.
    2. The hen sits on the egg to warm it.
    3. The baby chick pecks at the shell.
    4. The chick hatches from the shell.
G. 1. chicken   2. hatch
    3. pecks
H. 1. A   2. T   3. A   4. T
    5. T
I. (Suggestions only)

8 Kites

A. 1. Kites.
    2. Boxes, diamonds, dragons and more.
    3. The sky.
    4. $5.00.
    5. 3 times.

C.

E.
```
B D U X C O L V M T R S V A V K M F H
Q C F H I E V A L E N T I N E G I L K
T V I O L I N W F S V A N Z S T U R S
L A I R A I N R R E T B E O T O V R N
```

F.
1. Buy the paper, sticks, glue, and string.
2. Cut the paper, sticks, and string.
3. Glue the sticks and string to the paper.
4. Fly the kite.

G. (Suggestions only)

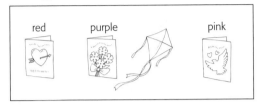

red   purple   pink

H.
1. teacher
3. nurse ; people
5. police officer
2. fireman
4. baker

Review 1

A.
1. We asked our mom for an old blanket.
2. We got some clothespins.
3. We took everything out to the backyard.
4. We pinned the blanket to the clothesline.
5. We are cozy inside our tent.

B.
1. c
2. s
3. t
4. d
5. b
6. m
7. f
8. r
9. g
10. p
11. w
12. j
13. h
14. n
15. k

C. (Suggestions only)

D.
```
K Y S U B B L M E S Z O D B F F A
U J X X C W N D H T F K P I Z Z A
U C C A R R O T H C O F D G E I U
D Y K H M O G U J L O X A S N Z E
E E O G S S K I T E T S C A T H L
U S T H H F G I H T X Y M F E V O
O F L O W E R R U G U U D S N D C
K N D G C E S K F M T R W S T S D
H E A R T T O E U E C B D O G F S
L S Y O M C U K F E U J C C O N D
D Y G O A T E C A S F N A S C H W
P M S V G L T C O A B R G H S F E
R T S C M O O N O W I T C H O B C
S S K E Z Z N V H C A E N R O W T
A J U E F W P A W I O V B A L L P
C N E S T M D L C J A M Y N P H N
D T G W O G E N S E H T E R A O M
R F I E M O J T U S E C H V A N C
```

E.
1. a bee
2. cups
3. cats
4. socks
5. a fan
6. the moon
7. dogs
8. a pig
9. hats

F.
1. Bill went to the zoo.
2. We had fun at the park.
3. Will you go to the store?
4. How do you go to school?
5. My friend Kate plays with me.
6. When are you coming to my house?
7. There are lots of rabbits at the pet store.
8. The cake is baking in the oven.

9 Living at the Zoo

A.
1. A zebra.
2. At the zoo.
3. Lily and Luther.
4. Before Zoey was born.
5. Lie in the warm sun.

D.
☐ = blue
■ = red

E.
1. First, I colour my picture.
2. Next, I glue my picture to the construction paper.
3. Then I cut my picture out.
4. Finally, I hang my picture on the wall.

F. (Individual drawing)

G. (Suggestions only)
1. zoo
2. sand
3. bad
4. feed
5. he
6. tag
7. honey
8. mouse
9. free
10. fan

H.
1. zoo
2. store
3. South Africa
4. ocean
5. park
6. classroom
7. kitchen
8. farm

10 The Fox and the Queen

A.
1. Fox
2. Queen
3. queen
4. fox
5. wood
6. questioned
7. queen
8. palace
9. questions
10. cunning
11. palace
12. slept
13. box
14. crown jewels

B.
1. Late at night.
2. In the palace.
3. He questioned the queen.

E.
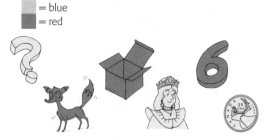
= blue
= red

F.
1. Put on a helmet.
2. Take the bike out to the sidewalk.
3. Put one leg over the top.
4. Place your feet on the pedals.

G. (Suggestions only)

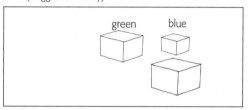
green   blue

H.
1. hat
2. hospital
3. clock
4. school
5. airplane
6. apples
7. bottles
8. boxes
9. cars
10. markers

11 The Wild Yak

A.
1. A large ox.
2. In Tibet.
3. Grass.
4. Black.
5. 1.8 metres.

C.

D.
1. I have a yo-yo.
2. I wind the string around my yo-yo.
3. I let the yo-yo fall.
4. My yo-yo goes up and down.

E.
1. A wild yak has long horns.
2. Your hat is in the box.
3. You have a pretty smile.
4. I need a yellow crayon.
5. The bird sings in a cage.
6. It is a yummy banana.
7. Look at my cute dog.
8. I like to play with my dog.

12 The Tree-house

A.
1. Robert.
2. A tree-house.
3. Some wood, some nails, and a hammer.
4. In the big tree (in their backyard).
5. In the summer.

B.
1. e   2. o   3. o   4. e
5. i   6. a   7. i   8. a
9. u   10. o   11. u ; e

C. (Suggestions only)

```
                              yellow    green    brown    you
```
(illustration: sun labelled yellow, tree labelled green and brown, girl labelled you, birds)

D.
1. The flowers are in bloom.
2. Where are my skates?
3. The dress is very pretty.
4. There are many bluebirds in the sky.

E.
1. down   2. above
3. large   4. tiny

13 The Bat

A.
1. mammals ; fly
2. country ; world
3. nocturnal ; hunt ; night
4. hearing
5. insects

B.
1. d   2. t   3. d   4. t
5. b   6. d   7. b   8. t
9. t

C. (Suggestions only)
1. b ; f ; m   2. b ; j ; r
3. b ; d ; m   4. b ; f ; h
5. l ; m ; t   6. b ; h ; k

D.
1. barked   2. start
3. playing   4. dancer
5. talks   6. name
7. baking   8. went
9. run   10. better

14 Making Blueberry Jam

A.
1. Pick blueberries.
2. A secret place.
3. They clean the berries and take out the leaves.

B.

C.　　(Individual drawing)

D.
1. soft
2. go
3. day
4. black
5. he
6. yes
7. sad
8. little
9. awake
10. they

⑮ Pretty Lights

A.
1. Pretty lights.
2. Night time.
3. The city.
4. (Individual answers)

B.

C.　　(Individual creation)

D.

	1		2		3		
	B		A	C	A	R	R	O	T
	A			A		A	
B	T	E	N	T		C	K	I	T	E
					E	

E.
1. rides
2. plays
3. looks
4. works
5. cooks
6. baked
7. walked
8. jumped
9. skates
10. likes

⑯ What Am I?

A.
1. a drum
2. the sun
3. a ball
4. a coin
5. a book

B.

C.

D	C	A	K	Y	G	U	O	M	X	H	D	F	V	I
E	U	B	L	N	P	E	W	Q	I	T	R	E	E	S
B	X	N	R	R	A	K	V	O	M	U	K	X	N	N
U	E	G	F	O	C	H	I	L	D	R	E	N	T	Y
C	S	J	U	X	O	M	J	D	E	T	A	U	R	B
N	Y	S	T	M	I	R	O	T	W	L	I	G	H	T
W	T	U	J	F	N	E	C	H	J	E	O	C	L	V
K	U	B	A	J	Y	F	L	C	N	S	E	V	O	I
T	X	K	L	A	V	C	N	E	D	B	G	H	P	S
U	T	T	O	M	O	R	R	O	W	S	C	L	O	D
R	E	O	F	B	C	A	C	L	E	V	Y	E	G	E
V	K	D	R	L	H	G	O	C	A	C	F	A	S	R
M	O	A	U	I	V	D	J	H	F	R	A	V	S	M
S	D	Y	N	C	S	C	H	O	O	L	U	E	B	I
T	A	V	B	A	T	J	S	P	L	D	T	S	U	A
E	D	I	F	V	O	T	N	S	L	X	N	H	O	Z
K	C	B	O	F	P	E	E	D	U	F	G	L	X	N

D.
1. pot
2. so
3. fun
4. bag
5. bed
6. rug
7. it
8. ran
9. hook
10. bake

⑰ Fun at School

A.
1. School.
2. Play games. / By playing games.
3. Teddy bear cookies.
4. Pictures.
5. She likes her school.

B.
1. c ; p
2. h ; t
3. b ; d
4. t ; p
5. b ; l
6. t ; t
7. d ; m
8. b ; g
9. b ; d
10. d ; r
11. p ; n
12. c ; t

C.

X	J	M	K	O	I	A	X	M	D	O	R	L
C	A	P	F	H	B	K	S	N	O	B	M	W
U	T	N	G	D	O	L	L	T	N	A	C	F
P	B	L	H	O	X	A	N	M	N	D	C	M
U	I	O	T	O	U	F	C	R	T	Q	J	Q
V	R	F	U	R	L	P	Q	D	V	W	W	F
X	D	B	H	T	A	A	F	R	J	B	A	G
T	N	G	D	H	U	N	Q	U	X	I	V	N
R	O	Y	X	A	M	P	C	M	O	B	H	B
S	T	E	N	T	J	Y	N	X	I	T	R	E
C	K	V	R	N	W	B	A	L	L	G	E	D
O	L	X	S	U	F	C	P	E	F	W	B	X
T	O	P	C	A	T	I	G	H	G	T	D	A

3. Cats ; (like) ; (play) ; yarn
4. Babies ; (cry) ; they ; (want) ; (fed)
5. Libby ; (drives) ; car ; work
6. David ; (plays) ; guitar
7. Kathleen ; (runs) ; track ; school
8. Rob ; (buys) ; cat food ; pet store
9. Christina ; (looked) ; mom
10. Ryan ; (rode) ; scooter ; sidewalk

D.
1. played
2. was
3. gave
4. will
5. wanted
6. rained
7. had
8. will
9. stopped
10. danced

Review 2

A.
1. Collecting rocks.
2. His mom.
3. From the Spring to the Fall.
4. On the sides of the roads and on paths.
5. Some have spots, some have stripes and others have many colours.
6. 123 rocks.

B.
1. a
2. i
3. e
4. a
5. u
6. e
7. i
8. o
9. u
10. o
11. e
12. i

C.
1. Ll
2. Yy
3. Zz
4. Qq
5. Yy
6. Zz
7. Qq
8. Ll

D.

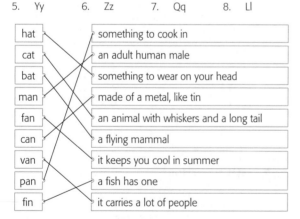

hat	something to cook in
cat	an adult human male
bat	something to wear on your head
man	made of a metal, like tin
fan	an animal with whiskers and a long tail
can	a flying mammal
van	it keeps you cool in summer
pan	a fish has one
fin	it carries a lot of people

E.
1. A book.
2. The sun.

F.
1. Go to the cupboard.
2. Get out a cone.
3. Get the ice cream out of the freezer.
4. Use a scoop to pick up the ice cream.
5. Put some sprinkles on top.
6. (Individual writing)

G.
1. boy ; (rode) ; bike ; store
2. kite ; (flew) ; sky